FANNIE LOU HAMER

FANNIE LOU HAMER

by June Jordan

Illustrated by Albert Williams

Thomas Y. Crowell Company   New York

CROWELL BIOGRAPHIES
Edited by Susan Bartlett Weber

Manufactured in the United States of America

L.C. Card 70-184982   ISBN 0-690-28893-X   0-690-28894-8 (LB)

1 2 3 4 5 6 7 8 9 10

KN JUN '73

FANNIE LOU HAMER

A CROWELL BIOGRAPHY

Fannie Lou's mother was short, Black, and
poor, in Mississippi, and she never let anybody
beat up on her babies. He could be big. He could
be white. He could be rich. But if he hit one of
her children, he was wrong. Fannie Lou's mother
would up and tell him so. Sometimes she had to
show him he was wrong.

There was that afternoon when the Bossman slapped her youngest boy. Fannie Lou's mother told the man to watch out about his heavy hands. He laughed in her face, and pushed her away from him. She held to his arm, and then, he attacked her, full force. She fought him right back, and he never bothered her kids, that heavy-handed way, again.

Some people worried about the mother of Fannie Lou Townsend. They figured that she must be crazy if she didn't have the sense to be afraid of white folks. But Mrs. Townsend was too busy to be afraid. And Fannie Lou wanted to be the same way, when she grew up: just too busy to be afraid.

Her mother did the laundry for the white man who owned the plantation where they lived. Fannie Lou would lie on the top of a pile of unwashed clothing, and watch her Momma, quietly.

Mrs. Townsend used a scrub-board that put blisters on the knuckles of her hands. She would scrub the clothes and sing to her baby girl, a sad, slow song:

> Sheep-eye Sheep eye
> where yo' little lamb?
> Way down in the valley . . . .

Fannie Lou tried not to cry, but the tears came anyway. Her Momma's song made her feel lonesome.

Fannie Lou was the last child born to Jim and Lou Ella Townsend. She was born October 6, 1917. There were already fourteen boys and five girls in the family.

Those were days when nobody Black could vote in Mississippi. Those were days when nobody female could vote anywhere in the entire U.S.A. There were a whole lot of things wrong.

4

Fannie Lou's parents worked, and they worked hard, and they stayed poor. They made tons and tons of soft white cotton grow from the lovely dark earth around them. But none of this land ever belonged to them. And the owner paid them very little money for their toil.

He sat on his porch, as cool, and comfortable, and rich as he could be.

All the Black children living on his plantation were hungry, almost every day. Fannie Lou stayed hungry. Hour after hour, she dreamed about milk and cornbread and, maybe, Christmas morning, when they could have oranges and apples, as a special treat.

At last she got to be six years old. She was playing near a shack of old wood nailed together, and patched, on the roof, with tin. This was her home. The Bossman stopped his car. He said, "Honey, you go on out there with yo' Momma and yo' Daddy, and you pick thirty pounds of cotton, and I'll carry y'all to my store, and give you anything yo' heart desires."

Fannie Lou was excited. She ran out to the field. She made herself pick the thirty pounds of cotton.

That was a great lot of cotton for such a small girl to gather. But when she was done, sure enough, the Bossman brought her to his store.

This is what she pointed to: one can of sardines, a quarter-pound of cheese, and a gingerbread cookie called Daddy-Wide-Legs. The food made her so happy that she never stopped to think she had been tricked into working. Now that he knew, and her family knew, she could work, she would always have to work in the fields. But there would be no more treats to sweeten her work.

From then on, you would see a tiny little girl, dragging a heavy brown sack behind her, under the burning sun. That was Fannie Lou helping her family in the cotton field.

When the crops were in, Fannie Lou could go to school. She loved it. She had a funny teacher named Professor Thornton Layne. He would wear his shoes the right way, for a while. Then the heels wore down. So he would switch them to the wrong feet, and walk around like that, "to let the heels straighten out," as he would say. But he was a good teacher, and she tried hard to learn all she could from him. That way, she could see the smile come in his eyes.

She used to win spelling bees and recite Black

poetry to the grownups because she knew her teacher and her parents would feel proud. When she saw how happy she could make folks feel, she decided that she never wanted to let her people down, at all.

Her family was so poor, Fannie Lou soon had to help out, full-time. She had to leave school, at the end of the sixth grade.

After a twelve-to-fourteen-hour working day, all the Townsend children would circle close together, roast peanuts, and laugh themselves to stitches at their Daddy's jokes. Then they would bed down for the night on cotton sacks stuffed with dry grass, or corn shucks that rattled like flaps of paper if you moved in your sleep.

If Fannie Lou had a secret crush on a boy, and he said "hey," he'd have to chase her a mile and a half before she would answer him "hello." But, except for a crush, Fannie Lou was never shy.

From when she was really, really small, people would stand her on a table, and she'd sing out, sweet and clear:

> This little light of mine
> I'm gonna let it shine
> Oh, this little light of mine
> I'm gonna let it shine
> Let it shine
> Let it shine
> Let it shine . . . .

Later on, as a teen-ager, she would go around to her friends, and she would say, "Now what you think? Black people work so hard, and we ain' got nothin' to show for it. The white folks don't do nothin', and they be drivin' they cars, and wearin' fine clothes, and eatin' them some fancy ribs and grits. You know one thing: that ain' hardly right."

That was dangerous talk. And Fannie Lou's friends didn't want to hear too much of it. In Mississippi, Black people could be killed for thinking out loud. But Fannie Lou never gave up her questions. She was set on fighting the mean, deadly reasons why Black people suffered, from one month to the next.

Race hatred always made her angry. When she was seven years old, a white boy had come up to her and said she couldn't play with his sister anymore. "You a dirty nigger!" he had shouted at her. Fannie Lou had punched him in the mouth. But she had learned that white hatred was so powerful, she would have to use more than just her two fists to stop it.

When she was thirteen, a white man had poisoned and killed her family's favorite cow, Della. This was the cow that let all the Townsend children suck on her, to drink her milk. Fannie Lou never forgot the murder of her cow. Right then and there, she decided that, whatever it would take to overcome this white hatred, she would do that thing. But she had to wait many years before she could make her own real fight, for love, and freedom.

In the meantime, a very special person had his eye on her. Perry "Pap" Hamer was in love with Fannie Lou. When she and her Momma went down a row, planting cotton, he would plow the row next to them, as fast as he possibly could, hoping to catch up to them. But it seemed to him that they were always gone, or that he could never plow fast enough. Finally, he caught up with her, and they became friends, and when she grew up she became his wife. They have been married more than twenty years, since 1945.

Life was different with "Pap." He saw to it that they always had food. He would do anything and everything to take care of his Fannie Lou. In winter he'd shoot rabbits and squirrels, so they would

have meat to go along with the delicious hot potato salad that Fannie Lou whipped together once or twice a week. But they were still poor, and they were still living on a plantation in Sunflower County, still in Mississippi, where Mrs. Hamer had been born.

Then came the summer of 1962. College students and Black leaders from the North, and several freedom-fighting organizations joined together to change Mississippi. They were determined to make it into someplace where Black people would be just as free as white people.

1962 was when a white sheriff put a bullet in the head of a Black man because the man was on his way to register to vote. These were some scary times. Most of the Black people were afraid to try and vote. But Fannie Lou got up one morning, put on her shoes, and walked right into Ruleville, Mississippi, and she registered to vote. Ruleville was the nearest town to her house.

After this, trouble fell into her life like a hammer smashing on her head. The plantation Bossman told her to take her name off the voting register or she would have to leave his land. He warned her husband "Pap" that, if he went with his wife, they would lose all their furniture, and he would lose his job.

So Fannie Lou had to leave the plantation, by herself. She went out to her people, and she said: "They take me from my husband, and they take my house from me. But still, at the next election, I will be there, voting just as much as white folks vote." Now people began to listen to her. She became a leader.

Her bravery made them brave.

"Pap" was fired from the plantation. Neither he nor Fannie Lou could find work. They moved into Ruleville, the nearby town. There they lived in a house that was more like a bare closet than a home. Cars full of white men armed with rifles passed by their door, and followed them wherever they went. The white men cursed Mrs. Hamer.

She stayed angry, and she continued to call on her friends, and ask them to register and vote. And she prayed that she would never hate the men who hated her. She said, "Ain' no such a thing as I can hate anybody and hope to see God's face."

Then Mrs. Hamer traveled to a meeting outside the state. She hoped to learn new ways to teach people to vote. It was a long trip, and she went by bus. As she was coming back, the bus stopped in Winona, Mississippi, for a few minutes. Some of the Black passengers got out to stretch their legs.

At that moment, the Mississippi Highway Patrol came up and carried several Black people off to jail. Mrs. Fannie Lou was one of the group taken prisoner. Inside the jail, the Highway Patrolmen made two other Black prisoners beat her with a solid lead blackjack. Mrs. Fannie Lou screamed and she cried and she screamed. But they had no mercy.

The National Black leader, Dr. Martin Luther King, heard what was happening to Mrs. Hamer. He sent some of his staff to the jailhouse, immediately. They demanded the release of Mrs. Hamer.

After receiving emergency medical care, Mrs. Hamer went to Washington, D.C., and told what had happened to her because she wanted to vote. She told newspapermen, congressmen, and numbers of citizens.

The next summer was the Democratic National Convention, of 1964. Along with many other Mississippi Freedom leaders, Mrs. Fannie Lou went to the convention to form a new Mississippi Democratic Party, a party that would let everyone vote. Then the new party would make voting mean as much to Black people as to white people. At the convention, Mrs. Fannie Lou told about her pain, about her beatings because she tried to get Black people registered as voters.

When they heard her speak, all good people of America were shocked by her suffering. White people felt a deep shame. Everyone respected her. Thousands and thousands of people wanted to help her on to a freedom victory.

White people and Black people came down to
her house in Ruleville, Mississippi, and they
worked with her. They went out and found Black
people who were willing and able to vote, and
they drove them to the Courthouse, and helped
them sign their names on the voting register. This
work took years and years, and it is still going
on. But steadily more and more Black folks registered to vote in Mississippi. And more and more
Black folks began to be elected to public office.
Things were beginning to change for the good.

30

Across the country, colleges and universities invited Mrs. Hamer to visit them and tell them about the hunger and the hurt that burdened Black children in the South. Everywhere she went, the people's hearts were moved, and they asked her, "How can we help?"

Mrs. Fannie Lou never forgot the hunger she had known, for most of her life. She knew that children were still dying from hunger where she lived. She said, "If you give a hungry man food, he will eat it. If you give a hungry man land, he will grow his own food."

This was the idea, the dream, that she began to work toward. She called it Freedom Farm Cooperative. If ever there could be a "freedom farm," owned and worked by poor Black and white people, they would never be hungry again. They would plant food and harvest it. They would eat the food they planted. They would share everything they raised.

This would mean that people would not be working to make a profit. People would work together because they needed the same things. People would work for what they needed, instead of working for "money," or for "a boss," who might be somebody else. Now Mrs. Fannie Lou asked her friends, all around America, to give her money enough to open such a farm.

The money began to arrive. Folks were proud to be able to help her. On Mother's Day, in 1971, 176,000 white high school students went on a March Against Hunger, in Chicago, Illinois. Each student found a store owner or businessman who would be willing to donate so many cents for each mile walked. After walking miles and miles and miles, the students collected the dollars they had earned. Then they sent these dollars to Mrs. Hamer, for her Freedom Farm.

There was some beautiful farmland for sale, not far from Mrs. Hamer's home in Ruleville. So, she bought it—but not for herself. On the contract, beside the word *Owner*, she wrote: *The Freedom Farm Cooperative*. This means that the farm belongs to everyone who works on it.

Next, Mrs. Fannie Lou bought tractors and seed. The farm was ready to start. More than five thousand people came to work this land, and share the food that would grow from this earth. Freedom Farm Cooperative spreads for 640 acres. It is becoming more and more successful all the time, serving more and more poor folks who live near enough to know about it.

But there are thousands and thousands more poor people still living in Mississippi. And so Mrs. Hamer has not finished her fight. The problems of hurt and hunger are huge problems, but Mrs. Fannie Lou is just too busy fighting to be afraid of failure.

She says, "The Lord has helped me to help my people." People everywhere know that Mrs. Fannie Lou has helped to make human freedom real, for everyone. Today, if you stop by the house of Mrs. Fannie Lou Hamer, she will make you feel at home. You may see five or six Black men, listening to songs, as they rest in large chairs. On the floor, little children also listen, and they roll around and clap their hands to keep time. Teenagers on the porch join in the singing.

Other men and women crowd by the screen door. You will find old and young and Black and white people all come together in this one house that is the home of "Pap" and Fannie Lou. A lady is playing the upright piano. Mrs. Fannie Lou and a few friends are singing Gospel songs, as she plays. Her strong voice reaches down to the end of the block, and out into the world:

> Precious Lord
> take my hand
> lead me on
> let me stand . . . .

Her house is full of people and her heart is full of love. Nothing will ever kill so much love.

ABOUT THE AUTHOR

June Jordan was born in Harlem and grew up in the Bedford-Stuyvesant section of Brooklyn. She studied at Barnard College and at the University of Chicago, and she has taught at the City College of New York, Connecticut College, and Sarah Lawrence College. A collection of her own poetry has been published, and she is the editor of two anthologies of Afro-American poetry. The recipient of a Rockefeller Foundation fellowship in creative writing and of the Prix de Rome in environmental design, Ms. Jordan is currently working on her second novel, which takes place in Ruleville, Mississippi, where Mrs. Fannie Lou Hamer makes her home. June Jordan's first novel was *His Own Where.*

ABOUT THE ARTIST

After winning awards at New York City's High School of Art and Design, Albert Williams studied art at the School of Visual Arts, where he had received a three-year scholarship. Three years out of art school, he won a citation of merit at the well-known annual exhibit of the Society of Illustrators. FANNIE LOU HAMER is the first book he has illustrated. Mr. Williams lives with his wife and his two-year-old daughter, Tiffany, in Flushing, Queens; and he tries to get to the country as often as possible to satisfy his deep love of "rural land," which is reflected in his illustrations along with his great admiration of Mrs. Hamer.